HOT TOPICS

DANGEROUS AND DEADLY

CHRYSALIS CHILDREN'S BOOKS

Useful internet websites

Check these out to find out more about dangerous animals and plants:

http://www.kidzworld.com/site/p745.htm
Why do people eat a poisonous fish? Read about the puffer fish and more.

**http://www.enchantedlearning.com/subjects/amphibians/
poisonfrogstrawbprintout.shtml**
Learn more about poisonous dart frogs and print out a picture to colour.

http://www.orkin.com/education/insects1.htm
A low-down on the most dangerous insects. Make sure you can spot them!

http://www.nationalgeographic.com/kingcobra/index-n.html
Here you can learn all about the king cobra, one of the deadliest snakes.

http://www.ecopals.com/meat_eaters.html
Find out how meat-eating plants kill prey.

http://www.herb.lsa.umich.edu/kidpage/factindx.htm
Read all about fungus and mushrooms, or try some games and experiments.

http://www.oneworld.net/penguin/pollution/pollution_home.html
Learn all about pollution and how it's dangerous to us and our planet.

http://www.pbs.org/wgbh/nova/leopards/seeinggame.html
See if you can work out which sort of disguise each animal uses – either to hunt or hide!

http://www.idahoptv.org/dialogue4kids/birdsofprey/facts.html
Read all about winged hunters like eagles and hawks.

http://www.pbs.org/wnet/nature/enemies/
Watch a video of lions hunting down buffalo – click on a link at the bottom
right of the page to watch the video.

http://www.nationalgeographic.com/kids/creature_feature/0107/crocodiles2.html
Read all about crocodiles and watch a video.

http://www.bbc.co.uk/dinosaurs/
Check out everything you want to know about dinosaurs.

Written by Rupert Matthews
Illustrated by Peter Bull, Mainline Design,
Treve Tamblin and John Yates
Designed by Juan Hayward
Cover designed by Clare Sleven
Editor: Rasha Elsaeed

This edition published in the UK in 2003 by
Chrysalis Children's Books PLC
64 Brewery Road, London N7 9NT

British Library Cataloguing in Publication Data
for this book is available from the British Library.

ISBN 1 903954 75 4

Printed and bound in China

Contents

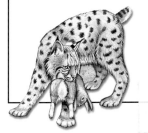

00984

The Japanese eat fugu fish. But if the wrong part of the fish is eaten by mistake, it is poisonous enough to kill.

Is there danger under the sea?

In Australia, a swimmer was stung by a jellyfish. He died just 30 seconds later!

S eas cover four-fifths of the world. In places, the sea is deeper than the highest mountain, Mount Everest, which is 8,708 metres high. Many strange creatures live in the sea, and some of them are very dangerous indeed.

Shark

Q Do any fish eat humans?

A Several types of shark will attack and eat humans. The most famous is the great white shark, which can grow to be over seven metres long. It can swallow a human whole! There are about 50 shark attacks on people each year, but because there is often no trace of the victims, the total may be much higher.

Q Do killer whales deserve their name?

A Yes. Killer whales (orcas), are the most dangerous of the toothed whales, and even attack whales which are twice as big as they are. They hunt in large packs and use many cunning tactics. They leap on to beaches to kill seals. Sometimes they find penguins and seals on ice floes. The whales push the ice floes to knock them into the water. Killer whales even smash their way through the ice to reach their prey.

Q Which is the most poisonous fish?

A The most poisonous fish in the world is the stonefish. When it lies on the bottom of shallow tropical seas, it looks exactly like a stone. If you step on it, the stonefish injects poison into your foot. The sting is incredibly painful. Most people die from the sting unless they receive treatment quickly.

Stonefish

Orcas sometimes attack boats. Perhaps they think they are other whales!

Q Which jellyfish is the most dangerous?

A Jellyfish kill their prey by injecting poison from their tentacles. Most jellyfish poison is very mild, but the sea wasp jellyfish can kill large animals, including humans and dolphins. Sea wasps live in seas around northern Australia and South-East Asia.

Sea wasp jellyfish

Orca

Q Why are sea urchins dangerous?

A Sea urchins are covered in long, sharp spines. These spines keep enemies away. Sea urchins are often found on underwater rocks. If you step on one, the spines can give a nasty wound. Some sea urchins have poisonous spines.

Sea urchin

Q Are any beautiful fish poisonous?

A The lionfish lives in the Pacific Ocean. It is marked with beautiful bold stripes. It has long spines which carry a deadly poison. If a lionfish feels threatened by an enemy, it will jab at it with its spines. The poison is very painful. Several people have died after being stung.

Lionfish

Q Which tiny animal can sink ships?

A A coral reef is a rock-like object made up of tiny animals called corals, and their skeletons. Reefs lie just beneath the surface of the sea, and may be several kilometres long. If a ship hits a reef, it can be ripped apart and will sink in minutes.

Coral

The fire salamander has a poisonous skin. People used to believe that this protected it from flames.

Are any frogs poisonous?

Fire salamander

Frogs are amphibians – cold-blooded creatures which usually live on land and breed in water. Amphibians secrete an unpleasant-tasting liquid from their skin, which helps to keep enemies away. In some types of frog, this liquid is poisonous.

Q How do humans use frog poison?

A The most poisonous frogs live in South and Central America. Some peoples collect the frogs and bake them to remove the poison from the skin. The concentrated poison is then smeared on arrows used for hunting and warfare. A single scratch from such an arrow can kill.

Q Which is the most poisonous frog?

A The golden arrow-poison frog may be the most dangerous frog in the world. It is about four centimetres long. If a small animal eats a golden arrow-poison frog, the poison will kill it. A larger animal will become very sick.

Q Is the common toad poisonous?

A The common toad is found across Europe, northern Asia and North Africa. It usually hides from danger, but if it feels threatened, it produces a foul-tasting poisonous liquid.

Pleurodoles salamander

Common toad

Golden arrow-poison frog

The first person to report the Komodo dragon to scientists was a policeman who chased a subject to the island of Komodo in 1910.

Komodo dragon

Q Are any lizards poisonous?

A The gila monster is a lizard found in Mexico and Arizona. It can deliver a poisonous bite. The poison is produced in its lower jaw and emerges through holes near its teeth. The gila monster chews its victim to work the poison into the wound. If a human is attacked, he can usually shake the lizard off before much poison is absorbed.

Q Which toad frightens its enemies?

A The fire-bellied toad's back is coloured like a normal toad, but its underside is bright red with black spots. When it is attacked, the fire-bellied toad flashes its red underside to warn that it has a deadly poisonous skin.

Q What is the Komodo dragon?

A Komodo dragons live on the island of Komodo, near Java. They are enormous lizards which can grow to over three metres in length, or even longer. These ferocious hunters prey mainly on deer and pigs.

Q Which salamander is spiky?

A The pleurodoles salamander lives in southern Europe and North Africa. It is born with long ribs, which have very sharp ends. When the salamander has grown into an adult, the ribs poke through its skin to form sharp spikes, often surrounded by red patches of skin.

Komodo dragon

Fire-bellied toad

Gila monster

At Peshawar in Pakistan, one scorpion stung nine people, killing eight of them.

Are insects dangerous?

In the 1340s, a plague spread by rat fleas killed one-third of the people in Europe.

There are about a million different types of insect. Many feed on plants, but some prey on other insects and animals. Many insects spread deadly diseases. Some spiders have a painful bite. A bite from a scorpion can kill.

Tsetse fly

Q Which diseases are spread by insects?

A Insect bites can transmit many diseases. One of the most dangerous is sleeping sickness, which is spread by the tsetse fly. In parts of Africa where there are lots of tsetse flies, it is not safe for people to live there. Some mosquitoes spread malaria, a fever which sometimes kills.

Q Why are houseflies dangerous?

A Houseflies are found all over the world. Although they do not sting or bite, they can be dangerous. They feed both on fresh food, and on rotting food or dung. A fly landing on your meal may bring with it germs and dirt from its previous meal.

Housefly

Q Which insects suck blood?

A Mosquitoes and some flies bite humans to suck their blood. The blackfly is common on sandy beaches in North America and can give a very painful bite. Mosquito bites often make your skin come up in a red lump, which may become very itchy.

Mosquito

Locust

Red-backed spider

The red-backed spider of Australia likes damp places and often hides in toilets. It can give you a painful bite!

Q Which insects can destroy crops?

A Many different types of insect eat crops, but locusts may cause spectacular damage. Each locust can eat its own weight in food in a day. A large swam of locusts can destroy the crops of an entire country, causing a famine which kills many people. In 1889, a huge swarm containing 250,000 billion locusts covered 3,000 square kilometres in Egypt.

Q Why do Africans shake their boots?

A Scorpions are active at night. When dawn comes, they like to hide in a dark, warm place. Sometimes they crawl into boots or shoes. People in Africa usually shake their boots before putting them on in the morning, in case they contain a deadly scorpion. A scorpion sting can kill.

Q Which insects eat each other?

A Mantids are insects which hunt other insects. They sit completely still on a leaf or flower, and then grab passing prey. Mantids are so aggressive that they will eat each other, even their own mates.

Q What is found in bee stings?

A The stings of bees and wasps can be very dangerous. They contain chemicals that cause a very sharp pain. Some people are sensitive to these, and may become very ill if they are stung.

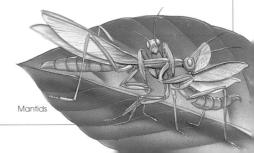

Mantids

The Australian taipan has enough poison to kill over 200,000 mice, its main prey.

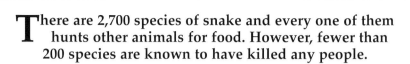

Are all snakes deadly?

Taipan

T here are 2,700 species of snake and every one of them hunts other animals for food. However, fewer than 200 species are known to have killed any people.

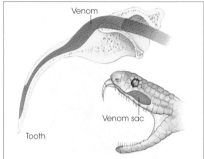

Venom

Venom sac

Tooth

Q Are all snakes poisonous?

A About 300 species of snake are venomous. There are about 100 species which kill their prey by constriction. This means the snake coils itself around its victim, slowly squeezing until the victim cannot breathe, and suffocates.

Q How do snakes inject poison?

A Some types of snake use poison to kill their prey. The poison, or venom, is produced and stored in a gland inside the skull, and is connected to the teeth. They have special hollow teeth which inject poison like a hypodermic needle. When a snake bites its prey, the poison runs into the wound and enters the animal's bloodstream.

Q How many people are killed by snakes each year?

A Snakes will attack a human only if they feel threatened or have been surprised, perhaps by being trodden on in long grass. It is thought that about 30,000 people die each year after being bitten by snakes.

Boa constrictor

The Indian cobra can spit poison to blind an enemy up to two metres away.

Cobra

Four times more men than women are bitten by snakes, because men spend more time working in fields.

Anaconda

Q Which is the world's largest snake?

A The largest snake in the world is the anaconda of South America, which is known to grow to about nine metres in length. But in 1907, explorer Percy Fawcett shot an anaconda which he thought was even longer: about 19 metres long. Unfortunately he did not have a tape measure to check this!

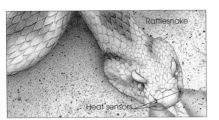

Rattlesnake

Heat sensors

Q How do rattlesnakes hunt in the dark?

A Rattlesnakes live in the Americas. They hunt rodents and other small animals. Just below their eyes, rattlesnakes have a pair of heat sensors. Using these sensors, a rattlesnake can find its prey even in total darkness.

Q Which is the thinnest killer?

A The vine snake lives in the forests of South America. It may grow to be 2.5 metres long, but is only about 1.2 centimetres in diameter. It preys on birds, but it will give a poisonous bite to any creature which disturbs it.

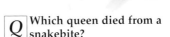

Vine snake

Q Which queen died from a snakebite?

A It is said that in 30 BC, Queen Cleopatra of Egypt was captured by the Roman army. She knew she would be executed and decided to commit suicide. She asked a servant to bring her an asp, because it was an ancient royal symbol. It was also a deadly poisonous snake, and Cleopatra knew its bite would kill her.

The sundew plant's sweet, sticky liquid attracts insects, and also dissolves them.

Where do poisonous plants grow?

Aethusa

Many different plants contain poisonous chemicals. Some plants use their poison to stop animals from eating them, but often the chemical is useful to the plant in other ways. Poisonous plants can be found anywhere. You shouldn't eat any plant unless it is known to be safe.

Q What is a Venus's fly-trap?

A A Venus's fly-trap is a plant which feeds on insects. It has special hinged leaves. When an insect lands on a leaf, it quickly folds up, trapping the insect. The plant then releases digestive juices which kill the insect and remove minerals from its body.

Foxglove

Q Can poisonous plants be used as medicine?

A Sometimes. For example, foxgloves grow all over Europe. They have large purple flowers and are often found in woodland. The leaves of the foxglove are very poisonous. Scientists can extract a chemical called digitalis from foxglove leaves, which is used to treat some types of heart disease.

Q Which common medicine comes from plants?

A In most homes, people keep aspirin tablets to cure headaches and other aches and pains. Aspirin is now made artificially, but was at first made from the leaves of a bush that grows in North America.

Venus's fly-trap

Aethusa looks like wild parsley, but is deadly if eaten, and has killed many people.

Adonis daisy

Acid from the Adonis daisy is used to treat heart disease, but is deadly if eaten raw.

Deadly nightshade

Q How do pitcher plants kill prey?

A Pitcher plants grow in tropical rainforests. They have cup-shaped leaves, which have a sweet liquid in the bottom to attract insects. Once an insect is inside the cup, it cannot escape because of the downward-pointing hairs in the cup. The insect drowns and is digested to provide the plant with minerals.

Pitcher plant

Q Are all berries edible?

A No. Berries are the soft, juicy covering of seeds. When they fall to the ground, berries provide the water and nutrients the seeds need to begin growing. Some berries are safe to eat and are very tasty. But many berries, such as deadly nightshade, are poisonous to humans. Never eat a berry unless you are sure it is safe.

Q Which stinging plant is good for human hair?

A The stinging nettle is covered with stiff hairs which inflict painful stings on any creature which touches them. However, the juice of the stinging nettle is said to help human hair grow strong and healthy.

Nettle

Artist's impression of a ya-te-vau

Q Is there a man-eating tree?

A In the 1880s, explorers in Central and South America reported a tree-like plant called the ya-te-vau. When an animal brushed against its branches, they would wrap around the victim, pricking its skin with spikes. The blood was then absorbed by the plant. It was said that a large tree would be able to kill a human. Despite many reports, no ya-te-vau has ever been seen by scientists.

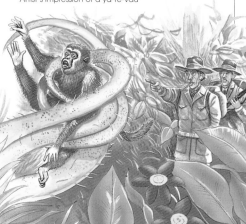

The rare and inedible Boletus purpureus turns bright blue if cut open.

Bo
pu

Toadstools are types of fungus which grow in many areas of the world. Some fungi are edible, but many are extremely poisonous. Nobody should eat any fungus unless they are expert at recognising which type it is. Many people die from eating toadstools.

Q Which fungus has got a dangerous twin?

A There are several types of morel fungus. The esculenta morel grows in woodland in the spring and tastes delicious. The false morel grows at the same time of year and looks almost identical, but is deadly poisonous.

Q Which is the most poisonous toadstool?

A The death cap toadstool gets its name because most people who eat it die. The death cap is a white toadstool with a pale bronze cap. It produces severe stomach pains about six hours after being eaten, and quickly destroys your liver and kidney. There is no known cure.

Destroying angel

Death cap

False morel

Esculenta morel

Q What is the destroying angel?

A The destroying angel is a rare, beautiful and deadly fungus found growing in woodland across Europe. It is pure white and smells sweet when cut.

The smelly stinkhorn smells like rotting flesh to attract flies which disperse its spores.

Stinkhorn

Artists often draw fairies with pretty red spotted toadstools. These fly agaric toadstools are very poisonous.

Q Which fungus kills trees?

A The honey fungus grows on deciduous trees, such as oaks and maples, in many parts of the world. If honey fungus spores land on a cut in a tree's bark, they will grow rapidly. Within a few months, the tree is dead, its wood rotted to white powder.

Q Which is the most valuable fungus?

A The most valuable fungus is the black perigord truffle which grows underground in Europe. It has a delicious and unique flavour. Its price varies during the year, but can be as much as ten times the price of pure silver.

Q Which is the most edible group of fungus?

A Nearly all the types of boletus mushroom are edible. The penny bun boletus, or cep, is harvested by mushroom farmers to sell. However, the devil's boletus is poisonous.

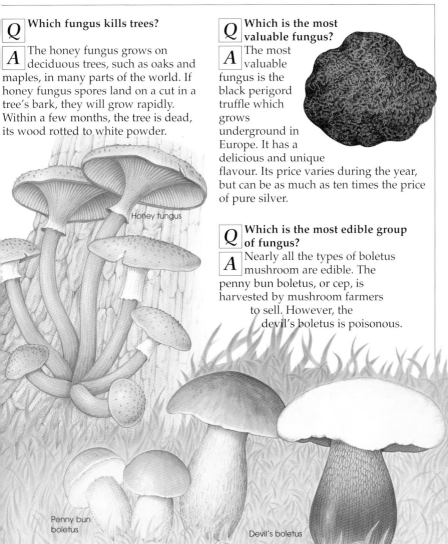

Honey fungus

Penny bun boletus

Devil's boletus

Methane gas produced by rubbish tips may cause explosions.

Is our environment dangerous?

The planet Earth and the atmosphere which surrounds it contain many dangerous and deadly substances. Some of these are very rare, but others may be found quite frequently.

Q What is a Will-o'-the-Wisp?

A In the past, people believed that the strange lights sometimes seen over marshes, were evil spirits, known as Will-o'-the-Wisp or Jack Lantern. They were thought to carry lanterns to lure travellers from safe paths to dangerous ground. In fact, the strange lights are caused by phosphine gas given off by rotting plants, which sometimes ignites suddenly.

Will-o'-the-Wisp

Q Why is granite dangerous?

A In some areas of the world, towns are built on granite rocks. Granite is slightly radioactive and gives off small amounts of radon gas. People who live there may breathe more radon than others, and it is thought that this may be dangerous over a long period of time.

Q Which water-holes are dangerous?

A Nineteenth-century explorers sometimes came across desert water-holes with poisonous water. Minerals such as alkaline salts and arsenic from nearby rocks would collect in the water-holes, poisoning the water. Such water-holes are now posted with warning signs.

Q Which gas kills miners?

A Mines dug deep underground disturb pockets of gas trapped beneath the earth. One of the most common of these gases is methane, which has no colour or smell. A spark or flame will cause methane to explode, so smoking and naked flames are banned in mines.

Explosion in a mine

ead is no longer used
o make water pipes,
because it can
contaminate the water.

Coal dust can cause
lung disease in
miners who breathe
it for many years.

Q Can rain be harmful?

A Some industrial processes give off dangerous gases. Sulphur gases cause acid rain, which may kill trees and wildlife. Acid rain erodes (wears away) stone, endangering historic buildings.

Q Where does the ground swallow people?

A Quicksand forms where water mixes with sand. Any object on the surface will gradually sink. This may also happen in peat bogs. In some places, the disappearance of several people has been blamed on peat bogs.

Q Why do mountaineers carry oxygen tanks?

A Mountaineers who climb to the tops of very high mountains need to take tanks of oxygen with them because the air is very thin above 7,000 metres.

Q Where is the air poisonous?

A Hot gases of sulphur and other poisonous gases sometimes seep from the ground near volcanic areas. In the Rocky Mountains in North America, there is a gorge which sometimes fills with sulphur gas, killing any animals that are in it.

The Bermuda Triangle

Q What is the Bermuda Triangle?

A Some people believe that parts of the world have supernatural powers. The Bermuda Triangle is an area of sea off Florida. Many ships and aircraft have vanished in this region. There may be a natural explanation for this, but nobody has found it yet.

Q Which dangerous gas comes from cars?

A Car exhaust contains a poisonous gas called carbon monoxide. Carbon monoxide is fatal if it is inhaled over a short period in a confined space. Exhaust also contains lead from petrol which is harmful to humans. We can help reduce pollution by fitting cars with a catalytic convertor, which helps to get rid of poisonous gases.

The arctic skua chases other birds to make them drop fish they have caught.

Which are the polar predators?

Arctic skua

The vast areas around the North and South Poles are very cold. The land and sea may appear to be bleak and empty, but many animals live there. Some of them are powerful hunters.

Q Which is the most powerful polar hunter?

A The polar bear is the most powerful and aggressive animal in the Arctic. It grows to be about 2.5 metres long, though some reach over three metres. Polar bears are very strong and hunt seals, fish and even reindeer.

Q Which polar predator changes colour?

A During the summer, a stoat has a reddish-brown coat. This allows it to hide from its prey on the tundra (the area between the polar ice cap and where trees start to grow). In winter, its coat turns white, with a black tail-tip, so it can blend into the snowy background

Polar bear

Q Which seal hunts penguins?

A The leopard seal gets its name because it has a spotted coat and is a fierce hunter. It likes to lurk beneath the ice of the Antarctic, waiting for penguins to dive into the water. When a penguin is within reach, the seal grabs it in its powerful jaws. Leopard seals are about 3.5 metres long.

Leopard seal

The stoat kills by leaping on its prey.

Stoat

Polar bears smash through the ice to reach sleeping seals.

Musk oxen

Q How do musk oxen protect themselves?

A Musk oxen are shaggy sheep-like animals which live on the Arctic tundra. When a pack of wolves approaches, the musk oxen bunch together in a circle with their horns facing outward, and their young in the middle. The wolves cannot break through this barrier, and usually go away.

Q Which hunter travels a long way in search of prey?

A The albatross hunts fish and crustaceans (creatures with hard shells) in the seas around the South Pole. It travels over the seas for months at a time, only coming to land to lay eggs. An albatross may fly over 80,000 kilometres each year.

Albatross

Walrus

Emperor penguin

Q Which predator eats only shellfish?

A The Arctic Ocean is home to vast numbers of shellfish. Walruses, which grow to over 3.6 metres long, eat shellfish. Walruses live in large herds, but hunt on their own. They have long tusks. Nobody is quite certain how a walrus eats its prey, but it seems to suck the fish out of their shells.

Q What does the largest penguin hunt?

A The largest penguin is the emperor penguin, which stands one metre tall. It has a long, slender bill which is good for catching slippery prey. Most of the time it hunts squid, and occasionally takes fish or other sea animals.

The flower mantis looks exactly like a flower, but it kills insects which come within range.

Are there dangers in disguise?

Flower mantis

Many hunting animals disguise themselves. This allows them to get closer to their prey and so stand a better chance of making a kill.

Q Which hunter uses a 'worm' as bait?

A The alligator snapping turtle lies on the beds of rivers and lakes in North America with its mouth gaping wide open. When a fish swims past, the turtle wiggles its tongue, which looks just like a struggling worm. If the fish approaches, the turtle snaps its mouth shut on the unfortunate victim.

Alligator snapping turtle

Q Which snake is almost invisible?

A The eastern green mamba lurks in trees in southern Africa. Its bright green colour is identical to that of the leaves on the trees where it lives. This makes the mamba almost impossible to see, unless it moves.

Q Which larvae catch ants?

A Ant-lion larvae feed on ants and other small insects by setting a clever trap. The larva digs a tunnel in sand and buries itself at the bottom. To a passing ant, this appears to be just a small hole. But if the ant climbs into the hole, it is pounced on by the waiting ant-lion larva.

Ant-lion larva

Q Which spider opens a door?

A Trapdoor spiders take their name from the way they catch their food. They dig a tunnel and make a door at the surface end. The door is made of silk mixed with sand and soil. The spider waits just beneath this door. When its prey walks past, the spider leaps out and grabs its victim.

Trapdoor spider

Hover flies are coloured yellow and black to look like wasps, but they cannot sting.

Hover fly

The Champawat man-eating tiger killed 436 people in India.

21

Eastern green mamba

Q Which fish electrocutes its victims?

A The electric ray buries itself in mud at the bottom of the sea. When a small fish comes near, the ray emits a powerful electric charge to stun the fish, allowing it to be eaten with ease.

Q Which great cat has a coat which allows it to hide in the shadows?

A The tiger hunts its prey through dense jungles and grasslands. Its striped black and orange coat helps it to merge into the bright sunlight and dark shadows of its home. A tiger stalks slowly through the undergrowth until it is close to its prey. Then it springs and kills the prey with a bite to the throat.

Q Which fish goes fishing?

A The angler fish lies on the bottom of the sea, partially buried in sand. It has a spine over its mouth which it uses like a fishing rod. On the end of the spine is a flap of skin, which looks like a worm. This acts as bait, and is waved about to attract small fish. When its prey is near, the angler opens its huge mouth, sucking its meal inside.

Electric ray

Angler fish

Gannets dive into water from a height of 30 metres to catch fish.

Are there winged killers?

Gannet

Many different types of bird and bat fly in search of prey. Some, such as swallows and bee-eaters, which eat insects, catch their prey in flight. Others swoop from the sky to catch prey on the ground. Both techniques require superb eyesight and great flying skill.

Q Which is the heaviest flying hunter?

A Condors, which fly in the Andes mountains of South America, weigh up to about 12 kilogrammes and have a wingspan of 2.8 metres. Condors feed mainly on carrion (dead animals), but are also thought to take small mammals.

Andean condor

Monkey-eating eagle

Q Which eagle hunts in forests?

A The monkey-eating eagle of the Philippines is one of the largest eagles. It is about 80 centimetres long, with short, powerful wings. These are small enough to allow it to dart through branches in search of the monkeys and other mammals on which it feeds.

Falcon

Q Which birds hunt on beaches?

A The great skua of the North Atlantic Ocean finds much of its food on beaches and close to the coast. It also hunts further inland. Skuas hunt the eggs and chicks of other sea birds, and attack any crabs or shellfish which they can find. Many gulls hunt on beaches too.

Great skua

Q Which birds hunt other birds?

A The most successful bird-killers among the birds of prey are falcons. They catch small birds by chasing them at high speed. Falcons can twist and turn while flying flat-out. They dive on larger prey from above.

The black skimmer flies with its lower beak in the water, hoping to strike a fish.

Black skimmer

King vulture

Q How do bats find insect prey?

A Most bats fly about to hunt insects. They find their prey in the darkness of night by using a form of sonar, called echo-location. The bat makes high-pitched clicking sounds which bounce off objects. It can tell the size and position of an animal by its echo, and can then home in for the kill.

Vampire bat

Q Which bat sucks blood?

A Vampire bats are about ten centimetres long, and live only in South America. They hunt at night, landing close to their prey and then crawling forward. They bite their victims and then use their tube-shaped tongue to suck up blood.

Q Which birds have the best eyesight?

A Eagles and hawks have good eyesight to enable them to catch their prey, but the sharpest eyesight probably belongs to vultures. These birds soar about 2,000 metres above the ground, looking for food. Even from this height, the birds can see a decaying carcass and swoop down to feed.

Bat using echo-location

Q How do dragonflies hunt?

A Dragonflies prey on other insects, usually gnats and flies. They have very good eyesight and can spot a flying insect 40 metres away. The dragonfly swoops on its prey, using its legs to catch it, and kills it with a single bite.

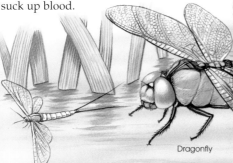

Dragonfly

Pronghorn antelopes can run as fast as 56 kilometres an hour to escape hunters.

Pronghorn antelope

Why do lions rule the plains?

The lion is the largest and most powerful hunter on the African plains. It may grow to reach three metres in length and weigh 300 kilogrammes. Few animals are able to survive an attack by a lion.

Lion

Lioness

Elephant

Q How do elephants protect themselves?

A On the African plains, elephants live in herds of up to fifty animals. Although fully-grown elephants are too large to be hunted by lions and leopards, young calves are in danger of being attacked. If a predator is seen, the older females will charge forward, trumpeting loudly, to drive it away.

Q How do lions hunt?

A Lions prey on zebras, gnu and various antelopes. They also eat birds and other small animals if they are very hungry. Lionesses do most of the hunting, working together to drive prey towards a place where the other lions are hiding.

Q What is a pride of lions?

A Lions live in family groups called prides. Each pride is made up of an adult male, up to fifteen females (lionesses) and their young, and sometimes young males too. The pride lives and hunts together.

Hyenas have jaws strong enough to snap and devour a buffalo thigh bone.

Lions make a kill on only one-third of their hunts.

Q Which animal steals meat from lions?

A After lions have made a kill, they feed immediately. Sometimes, hyenas try and steal their food. A large pack of hyenas can drive a small number of lions away from a carcass.

Kangaroo

Hyena

Q How do kangaroos fight?

A In Australia, kangaroos live on the open plains and are able to flee very quickly when danger threatens. However, when they cannot escape by running, kangaroos will lash out with their powerful hind legs. A single kick can knock a dog unconscious.

Rhinoceros

Q Why are rhinoceroses dangerous to humans?

A Rhinoceroses eat plants and do not hunt other animals, but they can still be very dangerous. When a rhinoceros feels threatened, it will lower its head and charge. The long horn on its forehead is a very dangerous weapon, especially because there is two tonnes of angry rhino behind it!

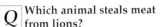

Grizzly bears sometimes rear on to their hind legs to reach food.

Which killers lurk in the woods?

Forests can be dark, forbidding places. Undergrowth may conceal a large animal and strange sounds echo through the trees. Hunters which lurk in the forests are among the most powerful in the world.

Q Which is the most powerful killer in the forest?

A The grizzly bear of North America is a huge and powerful hunter. It is usually about 2.5 metres long, but some grow to over three metres. They hunt fish and kill large deer and bison if they get the chance. Grizzlies usually avoid humans, but have been known to kill them.

Q Are any forest mammals poisonous?

A The short-tailed shrew of North America can deliver a venomous nip. It hunts vast numbers of worms, insects and small mammals, which are injected with fatal poison from its lower incisor teeth.

Short-tailed shrew

Q What is a bobcat?

A The swamps and forests of North America are home to the bobcat. Bobcats are about one metre long and have a beautiful spotted coat. They used to be hunted for their fur. Bobcats prey on rabbits, rats and other mammals.

Bobcat

Grizzly bear

Q Which killer is called the glutton?

A The wolverine of North America is known as the glutton (meaning greedy) because of its habit of killing more than it needs, and storing the food in snow. An adult wolverine can kill a reindeer and will return to the carcass many times until it has all been eaten.

Wolverine

Leopards carry their prey into trees to eat undisturbed.

Bobcats often hook fish from streams with their front paws.

Red fox

Q Which forest hunter also lives in cities?

A The red fox is found across Europe, Asia and North America. It usually lives in forest areas, where it hunts rabbits, birds and insects. However, in recent years, the red fox has begun to live in cities where it preys on garden birds and raids dustbins for food scraps.

Q Which forest hunter kills silently?

A Leopards are famous for their ability to glide silently through the night. They use this skill to creep close to prey and seize them in their jaws. In 1922, a leopard killed a man so quietly that a second man, sitting just two metres away, heard nothing at all.

Q Which is the rarest forest killer?

A This may be the Tasmanian wolf of Australia, if any still exist. The Tasmanian wolf is about the size of a big dog, up to about 1.3 metres long. It preys on kangaroos and other medium-sized creatures.

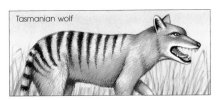

Tasmanian wolf

Q What is the Tasmanian devil?

A The forests of Tasmania in Australia are home to a creature which earned itself the name Tasmanian devil, because it fights savagely when cornered. This stocky, muscular creature is about one metre long and preys on birds, lizards and other small animals.

Tasmanian devil

Leopard

Crocodiles often store meat under sunken logs, returning when the flesh has begun to rot.

Is there danger in the river?

Many river animals live by attacking and eating other creatures. Some eat almost everything in sight, preying on anything they can reach. Only a few are able to kill animals as large as a human.

Q Which crocodile is most dangerous to humans?

A The salt-water crocodile of Australia and South-East Asia can grow to reach 5.5 metres in length. These crocodiles frequently attack any humans they come across. During the Second World War, about 900 Japanese troops were trapped in a swamp. After an attack by several crocodiles, only 20 of the men were left alive.

Salt-water crocodile

Q Which river fish can reduce an animal to bones in minutes?

A Piranhas are small fish with razor-sharp teeth, found in the rivers of South America. They live in large groups. Piranhas are very aggressive, and if they scent blood, they will even attack large animals. Humans can be reduced to skeletons in minutes.

Q What is the 'death roll' of a crocodile?

A Crocodiles have simple jaws which can only open and shut, not chew. When a crocodile grabs a creature too large to swallow whole, it will drag its victim to the bottom of the river and spin very quickly. This 'death roll' drowns the prey.

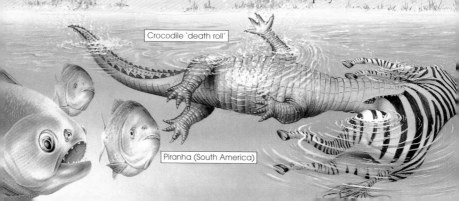

Crocodile 'death roll'

Piranha (South America)

The Ganges shark can attack people who bathe in the River Ganges in India.

Large pike drown ducks by gripping their feet and pulling them under the water.

Q Which insect eats fish?

A The most voracious hunter in European ponds is the nymph (larva) of the dragonfly. The nymph has long, clawed mouth-parts which it shoots out to spear prey. When it first hatches, a nymph preys on microscopic creatures, but eventually it will spear tadpoles and small fish as food.

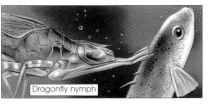

Dragonfly nymph

Q Which fish 'shoots' its prey?

A The archer fish lives in the mangrove swamps of South-East Asia. It was given its name because it shoots a stream of water at insects resting on leaves near the water. The archer fish can hit insects up to four metres away, sending them tumbling into the water to be eaten.

Q How do crocodiles ambush prey?

A When deer or other animals approach a river to drink, they may be in danger. If a crocodile sees them, it swims underwater to within a metre of its victim, then rushes forward to grab the animal in its jaws.

Crocodile

Archer fish (South-East Asia)

Tyrannosaurus had teeth 15 centimetres long.

Can fossils reveal killers?

Tyrannosaurus teeth

Scientists who study the fossilised bones of ancient creatures are called palaeontologists. By studying these preserved bones, palaeontologists can work out how an animal lived and what it looked like. Different kinds of bones are found each year, so our knowledge is increasing steadily.

Q Which was the largest land hunter ever?

A The largest and most powerful predator ever to walk the Earth was the dinosaur *Tyrannosaurus rex*, which lived about 80 million years ago in North America. This creature was about 15 metres long and walked on its hind legs. Some people think that it ate carrion (dead animals) rather than hunting live prey.

Q Which dinosaur used a claw to kill?

A *Velociraptor* was a dinosaur which lived in North America about 75 million years ago. It was able to run very quickly on its hind legs. It killed other dinosaurs by gripping them with the claws on its front legs, and slashing with the large claw on each of its hind legs.

Velociraptor

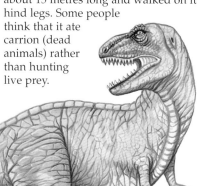

Tyrannosaurus

Dimetrodon

Q Which animal had a sail on its back?

A *Dimetrodon* was an early reptile which lived about 280 million years ago in North America. It had a tall fin, like a sail, on its back. The fin was used to absorb heat from the sun very efficiently. It used its long teeth to attack other reptiles.

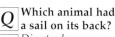

Ichthyostega

The first land predator with a backbone may have been Ichthyostega, an amphibian which lived 400 million years ago in Greenland.

Q Which giant bird hunted mammals?

A About 15 million years ago, *Phorusrhacus* stalked grasslands in South America. It was about three metres tall, and preyed on mammals and reptiles which it chased on its long, powerful legs. It had a large, hooked beak.

Phorusrhacus

Q What was the 'Jurassic tiger'?

A *Allosaurus*, known as the 'Jurassic tiger', was a powerful hunting dinosaur which lived about 140 million years ago in Australia, Africa and North America. It was 11 metres long and preyed on other dinosaurs.

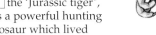

Allosaurus

Q Why did the sabre-tooth tiger have such large teeth?

Smilodon

A *Smilodon*, often called the sabre-tooth tiger, lived about 50,000 years ago in America. It used its extremely long teeth to stab the large mammoths and bison on which it preyed.

Q Which dinosaur hunted fish?

A In 1983, the remains of a flesh-eating dinosaur, called *Baryonyx*, were found in England. This dinosaur was about nine metres long and had a large claw on its front leg. Scientists think that the *Baryonyx* hooked fish with this claw and then secured them in its many small teeth.

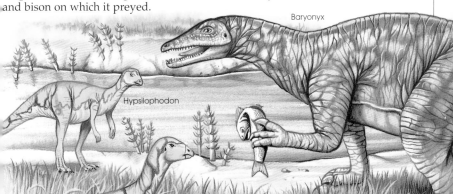

Baryonyx

Hypsilophodon

Index

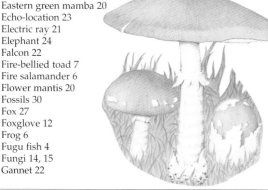